Dear Parent:
Your child's love of reading starts here!

Every child learns to read in a different way and at his or her own speed. Some go back and forth between reading levels and read favorite books again and again. Others read through each level in order. You can help your young reader improve and become more confident by encouraging his or her own interests and abilities. From books your child reads with you to the first books he or she reads alone, there are I Can Read Books for every stage of reading:

SHARED READING
Basic language, word repetition, and whimsical illustrations, ideal for sharing with your emergent reader

BEGINNING READING
Short sentences, familiar words, and simple concepts for children eager to read on their own

READING WITH HELP
Engaging stories, longer sentences, and language play for developing readers

READING ALONE
Complex plots, challenging vocabulary, and high-interest topics for the independent reader

ADVANCED READING
Short paragraphs, chapters, and exciting themes for the perfect bridge to chapter books

I Can Read Books have introduced children to the joy of reading since 1957. Featuring award-winning authors and illustrators and a fabulous cast of beloved characters, I Can Read Books set the standard for beginning readers.

A lifetime of discovery begins with the magical words **"I Can Read!"**

Visit www.icanread.com for information
on enriching your child's reading experience.

Clarence was just a muddy pickup.

One day, there was a big storm.

Lightning zapped the car wash.

Now Clarence has a secret.

Water turns him into Mighty Truck!

I Can Read Book® is a trademark of HarperCollins Publishers.

Library of Congress Control Number: 2016952352
ISBN 978-0-06-234467-0 (trade bdg.) — ISBN 978-0-06-234466-3 (pbk.)

18 19 20 21 22 SCP 10 9 8 7 6 5 4 3 2 1 ❖ First Edition

I Can Read!™

ON THE FARM

BY **CHRIS BARTON** ILLUSTRATED BY **TROY CUMMINGS**

HARPER
An Imprint of HarperCollinsPublishers

One day, Mighty Truck got a call.

"Hello?" he said in a mighty voice.

"Is that you, son?"

He switched to his Clarence voice.

"Mom! Dad!"

His mom spoke first.

"We have not seen you in so long."

"Please come visit," added his dad.

"Sure thing," Clarence said.

"I will see you soon."

A trip home to Mom and Dad's farm!
It was just the break he needed.

He really, wheely missed the place.

Clarence could go fishing.

He could romp with the sheep.

He could play with the pigs.

He could rest and relax.

But Mom and Dad had other plans.

They needed help with the farm.

So much for romping and playing.

So much for resting and relaxing.

And fishing? Forget it.

First Clarence mended a fence.

After that, he hauled loads of beets.

Next he planted rows of corn until dark.

But Clarence still had lots to do.

He needed some help himself.

And he knew just how to get it.

Clarence got up before the sun rose.

He rolled over to the well.

"This should do the trick!"

He gave the handle a bump.

Water began to pump.

Clarence splashed in it.

And Clarence became Mighty Truck.

"Who?" said the barn owl.

"Shhh," shushed Mighty Truck.

What chore would he do first?

Mighty Truck saw the field.

"All right, let's go!" he said.

"I have a lot of hay to mow."

ZOOM! He cut the hay mighty fast.

His heater got it mighty dry.

He pushed it into a mighty stack.

It was time to milk the cows.

But they were far from the barn.

The cows did not want to walk.

"No problem," said Mighty Truck.

"I will bring the barn to you."

It was time to get the chickens' eggs.

Mighty Truck rumbled along.

The eggs rolled around.

One egg hatched.

"Peep!" the little chick said.

Mighty Truck was mighty careful.

"Back to the nest you go," he said.

The sun was starting to rise.

Mom and Dad would be up soon.

Mighty Truck rushed to do more work.

He fed mules and scattered seeds.

He had to hurry.

Time to turn back into Clarence!

Mighty Truck raced to the haystack.

He drove right into it.

He came out covered in dirt and straw.

He was Clarence again.

And he headed back to bed.

But not for long.

Mom came into his room to wake him.

"Clarence, it is time to get up."

"That's right," Dad said.

"There is a lot of work to do."

"Are you sure?" Clarence asked.

They looked out the window.

His dad was surprised.

"How did all of that get done?"

His mom was amazed.

"And it's all been done mighty well!"

"There's nothing left to do," Dad said.

"Oh, yes, there is," said Clarence.

There was romping and playing.

There was resting and relaxing.

And, when Mom and Dad were not near?

There was some mighty good fishing.